Best-Ever
Activities for Grades 2–3

Grammar

Dozens of Activities With Engaging Reproducibles That Kids Will Love...From Creative Teachers Across the Country

BY JOAN NOVELLI

SCHOLASTIC
PROFESSIONAL BOOKS

New York • Toronto • London • Auckland • Sydney • Mexico City
New Delhi • Hong Kong • Buenos Aires

Thanks to the educators who contributed material for this book: Karen K. Bjork, Jackie Clarke, Cynthia Faughnan, Maryanne Frawley, Paula W. Hotard, Lyn MacBruce, Emily A. Olesch, Janice Reutter, Charlotte Sassman, Wendy Weiner, Judy Wetzel, Wendy Wise-Borg, and Janet Worthington-Samo.

"Commas" from Bing Bang Boing by Douglas Florian. Copyright © 1994 by Douglas Florian. Reprinted by permission of Harcourt Brace.

Produced by **Joan Novelli**
Cover and interior design by **Holly Grundon**
Cover and interior art by **Paige Billin-Frye**

ISBN 0-439-35529-X

CONTENTS

CONTENTS

About This Book

Whoever heard of having fun learning the rules of language? Well, with games like Beanillionaire and Punctuation Bounce, your students will be eager to master the skills that lead to correct writing and speaking. This book features both of these games (see pages 29 and 31), along with dozens of other activities and tips that will enliven grammar lessons and motivate students to learn punctuation, mechanics, sentence structure, and more.

The activities in this book are designed to help students grow in confidence and skill as writers and speakers. To support your instructional goals, the activities are aligned with the standards outlined by the Mid-Continent Regional Educational Laboratory (MCREL), an organization that collects and synthesizes noteworthy national and state K–12 curriculum standards. These standards suggest that students in grades 2 and 3 use the following grammatical conventions in their writing: various sentence types; nouns, verbs, adjectives, and adverbs; and conventions of capitalization and punctuation.

This book can help you provide instruction in those areas through activities that connect with other curriculum areas and tap into the many ways students learn. For example, Adjective Detectives puts a scientific spin on language lessons as students use attributes to try to identify the hidden object in a sock. (See page 12.) In Noun Walk-Around, students explore parts of speech in the world around them. (See page 10.) And in Punctuation Bounce, a ball gives students a hands-on lesson in using end punctuation and capital letters. (See page 31.) Other features include:

- ideas from teachers around the country
- activities that correlate with the language arts standards
- lots of reproducible activity pages, including poetry, games, graphic organizers, mini-books, and more
- literature connections
- multiple-intelligence links, with suggestions for integrating art, writing, movement, and music
- strategies for second-language learners

- test-taking and assessment tips
- suggestions for interactive morning messages
- take-home activities to involve families in student learning
- and many more activities that involve kids in moving, writing, speaking, collaborating, creating, thinking, playing, and more, as they strengthen grammar skills!

What's My Noun?

This guessing game gets children writing and guessing as they identify nouns by examining attributes.

○ Write "What's My Noun?" at the top of a sheet of chart paper or a white board. Cut a slit in the top of a shoe box and place it next to the display.

○ Write various nouns on slips of paper and place the papers in a bag. Or, for a more concrete version, place actual objects in a bag.

○ Invite a child to choose a noun from the bag and then describe it (without naming it) on the chart paper or white board. For example, the child might describe the noun's shape, color, and size, and tell, what it's used for.

○ Have students guess the noun, write it on a slip of paper, and place it in the box. At a designated time, let the child who created the list read students' guesses and reveal the noun.

○ Repeat daily to give additional children a chance to describe nouns for the class and to let students become more skilled at identifying specific nouns—for example, basketball instead of ball.

Maryanne Frawley
Amery, Wisconsin

For a partner version of this activity, let children choose a noun to describe. Then pair up children and let them make and trade lists of words that describe their "secret" nouns. Can they guess each other's nouns?

Literature LINK

A Mink, a Fink, a Skating Rink: What Is a Noun?

by Brian Cleary (Carolrhoda Books, 2000)

"Hill is a noun. Mill is a noun. Even Uncle Phil is a noun." Rhyming text and lively illustrations zip readers along in this out-of-the-ordinary lesson on nouns. Children will have fun substituting their own words for those in the book to learn more about nouns and make new rhymes.

Rhyming People, Places, Things

Let children draw inspiration from Brian Cleary's *A Mink, a Fink, a Skating Rink: What Is a Noun?* to create their own sets of rhyming nouns. The wordplay is pure fun, but students will get plenty of practice with word choice, too.

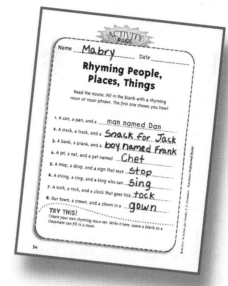

Find more than 15,000 words in *The Scholastic Rhyming Dictionary*, by Sue Young (Scholastic, 1999), a kid-friendly resource organized by vowel sounds and final syllables.

After sharing the book, invite students to brainstorm nouns that rhyme. How about a home, a dome, and a gnome from Rome? After sharing some ideas, give students copies of page 34. Have them complete each set of rhyming nouns by filling in the blanks. Then invite them to make up their own sets of rhyming nouns. A rhyming dictionary will come in handy and help broaden students' thinking about their word choices. (See Tip, right.) Have students choose three or more rhyming nouns and then write their words on drawing paper and add illustrations. Put the pages together to make a book, or use them to create a colorful collaborative banner that wraps around the room.

Literature LINK

The Letters Are Lost

by Lisa Campbell Ernst (Viking Penguin, 1996)

In a book about lost letters, A is discovered in an airplane and B in a bath. "C joined a family of Cows. D was a Dog's tasty treat." Use the book to highlight nouns. (For each letter of the alphabet, the noun in the sentence is capitalized.) Then get ready for more with the book's ending: The letters are together again but not for long. Can readers guess where they're going?

Letters on the Move

Students write a sequel to a clever alphabet book to put a playful twist on what they know about parts of speech.

Share *The Letters Are Lost.* (See page 7.) After reading the ending, let students guess where the letters are off to now. Write each letter of the alphabet on a slip of paper and place them in a bag. Have children randomly choose a letter to write about in an innovation on the book. Students can use the book as a model for sentence structure and illustration (alphabet-block-style art).

Take-Home Activity:
Noun-a-Morphs

Children learn that nouns name people, places, and things, but things get tricky when it comes to capitalization. Try this "morphing" activity to have fun learning the difference between common nouns and proper nouns.

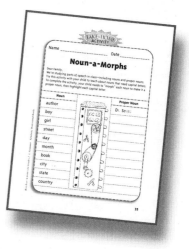

TIP

Children may have an easier time identifying nouns that are concrete, such as *child* or *school*. Help children recognize that sometimes a noun can also name a thing that is more abstract, such as *friendship* or *excitement*.

ⓖ Invite children to share what they know about nouns. Let them look around the room and take turns naming some nouns. Help students recognize that nouns name people, places, and things.

ⓖ Review what students know about using capital letters. If you use a morning message, have students identify words with capital letters and the kinds of nouns these words name. For example, the date names a thing, your signature names a person, and so on. (Note that using the morning message in this way is also an opportunity to point out other instances in which capital letters are used, including in greetings such as "Good Morning, Boys and Girls.")

ⓖ Give each child a copy of page 35. Ask children to share what they know about morphing, then explain that you want them to morph all the words in the first column to make them proper nouns. Read through the words in the first column together, and review what they have in common. (They're all nouns. They don't have capital letters.)

ⓖ Let children take home the pages and let their families help them morph each noun to make a proper noun. When children return their papers to school, let them take turns sharing the words they chose and the letters they capitalized.

Word-Building Inventions

This adventurous activity lets students put nouns together to design inventions.

Work with students to create a list of nouns on the chalkboard. Challenge students to put two or more words together to invent something new—for example, someone might put *sky* and *bicycle* together to create a *skycycle*, a bike that is ridden in the sky instead of on the ground. Invite students to sketch a design of their invention and describe in writing its purpose and benefits. Provide time for sharing and comments.

Jackie Clarke
Cicero Elementary
Cicero, New York

Nouns for Math Practice

Connect math and grammar by letting students add nouns to their math word problems.

Lots of math worksheets have word problems that involve somebody doing something. Somebody has apples to divide evenly among friends; somebody has money to buy candy and needs to know how much is left over; somebody wants to save money for something and needs to know how long it will take…. Problems like these are perfect for reinforcing parts of speech—in particular, nouns. Use a correction pen to white out any names, places, or things in the word problem. Let students read the problem and fill in words that make sense. They'll get practice capitalizing proper nouns and using context to figure out where names for people, places, and things belong.

Noun Walk-Around

This game lets students enjoy a walk outside as they notice and name nouns.

- Review the definition of a noun, then brainstorm a chartful of them. Ask students which of those nouns they might find on a walk around the school.

- Give each student a small paper bag to take on a walk. It will be helpful for students to bring notepads or clipboards and pencils.

- As they take their walk, have students notice objects around them—for example, tiny stones, leaves on the ground, small sticks, and pinecones. Before they put the objects in their bags, have them jot down a note about where they found it—for example, on the ground next to a tree.

- Back inside, have students take turns sharing their nouns. Spread out a large sheet of mural paper, and let students work together to create a mini-version of their walk. Have them glue their objects to the paper, then add details such as trees, leaves, and paths.

- To reinforce vocabulary, have students label the nouns in their mural. They can continue to add labels as they notice and name additional details in their artwork.

For a challenge, add a rule: Students can use up to but no more than three nouns from the same category—for example, no more than three names, three animals, or three fruits.

Alphabet Countdown

After studying nouns for a few days, try this timed activity to have some fun with nouns students know.

Give each student a copy of the record sheet on page 36. Ask children how many nouns they think they can name in three minutes (one for each letter of the alphabet). Let them make their guesses, then start the timer. At the end of three minutes, let students pair up and exchange papers. Have them put a star next to words they think are nouns and circle those they don't think are nouns. Have students take back their own papers and count the number of words that are nouns. If students can use as nouns any of the circled words on their papers, award extra credit. Repeat the activity another day. Can students increase the number of nouns they name in three minutes?

Cynthia Faughnan
Hartford Memorial Middle School
White River Junction, Vermont

Pronoun Bingo

Children put pronouns in their place with this variation on Bingo.

On slips of paper, write sentences that contain pronouns. Include subject (*I, you, he, she, it, we, you, they*), object (*me, you, him, her, it, us, you, them*), and possessive (*my, your, his, her, its, our, their, mine, yours, his, hers, its, ours, theirs*) pronouns. Give each child a copy of the Bingo board on page 37 and a handful of markers (such as dried beans). Write pronouns from the sentences on the chalkboard and have children copy the words on their boards, one word per square. Randomly select a sentence from the bag and read it aloud, leaving out a pronoun (inserting a pause in place of it). Have children listen carefully and decide if they have a pronoun that fits. If they have this word, have them put a marker on the square. Play until someone has five squares filled in across, down, or diagonally.

Advertising Adjectives

Students learn about words that describe nouns with an activity that also reinforces consumer skills.

- Invite students to bring in and share advertisements for favorite products—for example, food they like, games, and sneakers. If possible, tape a few commercials to view with students, too.

- Ask what all the materials have in common. Guide students to recognize that the ads try to get a person to buy something. Ask how the ads do it (by describing the product with lots of favorable words). Explain that the describing words advertisers use are called adjectives. They tell more about the product (a noun).

- Have students identify adjectives from the ads. List them on chart paper. Help students see that adjectives tell what kind, which one, or how many.

- Let students develop their talent in this field of writing by creating their own ads (or commercials) to sell a favorite toy or other product. (Students might like to work in groups for this.) Have them write an ad for the product and underline all the adjectives they use. Students can display print ads or perform commercials.

Janet Worthington-Samo
St. Clement School
Johnstown, Pennsylvania

Adjective Detectives

Students focus on word choice while stretching science skills with this interactive display.

Have students bring in odd socks. Tack the socks to a bulletin board, making sure there's one for each child, then have students choose a small object to hide in their socks. Give them all a chance to place the object in the sock without anyone looking. Make copies of the Adjective Detectives form on page 38 and give one to each child. Have children complete the form, writing three descriptive clues about the object in their sock (such as size, shape, and color) and then filling in the name of the object in the space provided. Show students how to make a flap to cover the name of the object by cutting a small piece of paper to size, placing it over the name, then taping only the top edge. Let students visit the bulletin board to guess their classmates' mystery objects. They can lift the flaps to self-check.

Paula W. Hotard
St. Philomena School
Labadieville, Louisiana

Literature LINK

Juba This and Juba That

by Virginia Tashjian (Little, Brown, 1995)

This playful collection of stories, songs, chants, poems, rhymes, and riddles includes the irresistible "What Did You Put in Your Pocket?" by Beatrice Schenk de Regniers. The poem begins "What did you put in your pocket/What did you put in your pocket/in your pockety pockety pocket/Early Monday morning?" The verse repeats for each day of the week, with an answer after each that ranges from "slushy glushy pudding" on Monday to a "spinky spanky handkerchief" on Sunday. The refrain cumulatively repeats what's in the pocket for each day of the week, so by the end students will be chiming in with a long list. For an innovation on the poem that strengthens the use of adjectives, let students take turns substituting something new for each day of the week.

Interactive Morning Message:
I Spy Adjectives

The detail-packed I Spy books are perfect for exploring adjectives. This morning message lets children go further by writing their own mini I Spy adjective riddles.

Share *I Spy Super Challenger*. (See below.) As children solve the riddles, take time to identify adjectives. Guide children to notice numbers that tell how many (*two* snowmen), words that tell what color (a *brown-and-white* dog), words that describe sizes (*little* glass heart), and so on. Display a picture from the book, along with a morning message that invites children to describe something they "spy." Have children write their mini I Spy riddles on the morning message and sign their names. Take time at your morning meeting to let children solve their classmates' riddles. Repeat the activity with other scenes from the book.

Literature
LINK

I Spy Super Challenger
by Jean Marzollo and Walter Wick (Scholastic, 1997)

I Spy fans will recognize favorite pictures from previous I Spy books, each with an all-new riddle. The scenes in this collection are among the most complex, and the new riddles that go with them challenge children to find some of the most difficult details—including plenty of objects to reinforce lessons on adjectives. "A little blue duck," "six red shoes," "ballet slippers," "a birthday candle," and "chocolate sauce" are just a few of the examples students come across in their I Spy adventures.

Adjective Olympics

Which student has the longest feet? Who can tell the funniest joke? Who's the fastest runner? Who's wearing the most colorful socks? Who has the strangest pet? Your students will make all sorts of interesting discoveries about their classmates with this Olympic activity.

- Make copies of the Adjective Olympics medal on page 39.

- Brainstorm with students adjectives that could describe something special about their classmates. These can be silly, strange, or serious (but always positive).

- Let students suggest a winner for first place in each category. Then, let each student complete and decorate a medal for another child; then hold an awards ceremony. Play some majestic music before bringing students up one at a time to accept their medals.

Adapted from *25 Great Grammar Activities,* by Bobbi Katz (Scholastic, 1999).

Literature
LINK

Hairy, Scary, Ordinary: What Is an Adjective?

by Brian J. Cleary (Carolrhoda, 2000)

"They're colorful, like mauve and puce. They help explain, like lean and loose." Playful rhymes and whimsical illustrations whisk readers from page to page to learn about adjectives. As an extension, reread the book and let students add on to each type of adjective that is introduced—for example, adjectives that describe or explain.

I'm an Adjective!
Mini-Thesaurus

This mini-thesaurus gets students using reference books as they explore descriptive vocabulary.

Give each student a copy of page 40. Have students fold the pages to make a book. Invite children to think of adjectives that describe them, then record them on pages 2–4 in the space provided. As a lesson in using a thesaurus, have students find and list synonyms for each adjective. To follow up, you might invite students to write descriptive paragraphs about each other, using the words in the mini-thesaurus.

Colorful Caterpillars Grow Long

This interactive display invites children to explore adjectives and adverbs as they create long, colorful caterpillars.

- Make two copies of the caterpillar face pattern on page 41. Enlist children's help in cutting out additional ovals from construction paper.

- After sharing a book with children, revisit a few sentences to identify adjectives and adverbs. Let children name other adjectives and adverbs on their own. Record some of their words on the ovals (one per oval). Gather students outside the classroom and put up the start of the caterpillar displays—tacking up one caterpillar "face" and adding on adjective ovals, then doing the same for the adverbs with the second caterpillar face. Add construction paper legs, two per oval. Reread the words with children.

- Continue to add to each caterpillar as students identify more adjectives and adverbs in books they read. Can students make their caterpillars stretch down the hall and around the corner? Passersby will enjoy seeing all the words and learning some colorful word choices for their writing.

Wendy Weiner
Parkview Elementary School
Milwaukee, Wisconsin

The *Scholastic Children's Thesaurus*, by John K. Bollard (Scholastic, 1998), defines synonyms. Illustrations provide visual clues and information boxes invite children to learn more.

Adjectives About Me

Students create self-portraits with words, learning more about themselves and becoming more skilled at choosing and using specific language.

After teaching adjectives, ask children to name adjectives that describe themselves and/or each other. Record suggestions on chart paper and display. Encourage children to be specific in their choices. Although *nice* might fit, stronger choices might be *helpful* and *cheerful*. Give children copies of page 42. Have children complete each section to describe themselves, then write their name at the bottom and make a paper flap to cover it.

Lyn MacBruce
Randolph Elementary School
Randolph, Vermont

TIP

These adjective self-portraits make great displays at open-school night. Parents will enjoy trying to spot their children by reading the adjectives they used to describe themselves.

SECOND Language LEARNERS

Cutting out pictures from magazines gives second-language learners a chance to learn language skills through multiple approaches—in this case, the activity provides both a visual and hands-on learning experience. Start by giving students a list of adjectives. Have them look for and cut out pictures that represent these words and then use them to create a collage. Have students copy the adjectives from the list on sticky notes and use them to label the adjectives in the picture. They can remove the words and repeat this part of the activity (and do the same with classmates' collages) to expand their vocabulary for and understanding of adjectives. For a more basic approach to this activity, start with an adjective such as *red*. Have children find pictures of things that are red and cut them out for their collages.

Dunk, Dive, Slide!

Students web sports verbs to practice using specific language to describe actions.

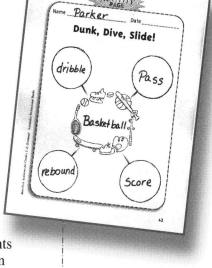

Take students outside or to another open space to play a game such as kickball or soccer. After they've had plenty of action, bring them back to the classroom for some wordplay. Draw a large web on the chalkboard. Write the name of the game in the center. Invite students to suggest action words that describe the game. Record these words on the web. If students suggest words that are related to the game but are not verbs, guide them to make another choice. As a followup, give students copies of the web template on page 43. Let them web action words that describe a favorite sport. (Students can draw inspiration from the sports pages, too.) Display webs on a bulletin board decorated with pictures of balls and other sports equipment.

Wendy Wise-Borg
Rider University
Lawrenceville, New Jersey

Literature
LINK

To Root, to Toot, to Parachute: What Is a Verb?

by Brian P. Cleary (Carolrhoda, 2001)

"Verbs are words like sing and dance, pray or practice, preach or prance, toss and tumble, jump and jam, whine and whisper, sleep and slam." This fast-paced book introduces action words (along with other kinds of verbs), and will lead to lots of fun followup activities. For example, have students add to the list of verbs above, suggesting pairs of verbs that use alliterative language. How about *leap* and *look, bake* and *beep, read* and *ride, swim* and *sweep*?

For a variation on the sports words web, invite students to think of a favorite activity. Have them write about it on a sentence strip, using verbs to tell about the action. Then invite them to draw pictures of themselves doing the activity.

Take-Home Activity:
Clap, Wiggle, Stomp

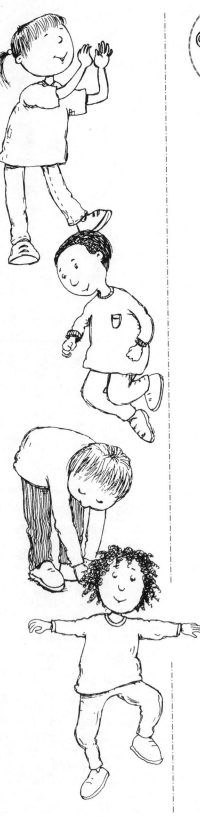

e familiar and favorite song "If You're Happy and You ow It" invites students to come up with actions for new ses—which means building their vocabulary of verbs.

Write the words to "If You're Happy and You Know It" on chart paper:

> If you're happy and you know it, clap your hands,
>
> If you're happy and you know it, clap your hands,
>
> If you're happy and you know it, and you really want to show it,
>
> If you're happy and you know it, clap your hands.

Ask students what the action is in the song. (*clapping*) Underline the word *clap* each time it appears. Then sing the song together and let children join in on the action.

Since one time through won't be enough, ask children what other verbs (or actions) they could substitute for *clap*. List their ideas— for example, *stomp your feet, wave your hands, touch your toes,* and *jump up high*—and then sing the new verses.

Let children share their action-packed song at home. Give them copies of page 44. In the spaces provided, have students fill in the verbs (or verb phrases) for new verses. Can they and their family members think of other actions? Take time to sing them in school.

Actions With Impact

This unconventional lesson lets students discover the impact of strong verbs on their writing.

- Surprise students in the middle of a fairly calm activity (such as a read-aloud) by acting out an unexpected and lively scenario— for example, you might pretend you saw a spaceship go by the classroom window or act very bothered by a nonexistent fly that won't leave you alone (stomp around it, swat at it, wave it away). Act out the scenario as dramatically as you can in order to give children lots of material to describe later on.

- After your theatrical experience, explain that it was just an act, then invite children to describe what they heard and saw. Record their comments on the chalkboard. ("You jumped from your seat and rushed to the window; you shouted for us to come, too; you pointed to the sky; you shrieked that there was a spaceship," and so on.)

- After soliciting a dozen sentences, have students identify the verbs in each. Then write as nondescriptive a sentence about the event as you can on the chalkboard ("I saw a spaceship") and compare it with students' sentences. Guide students to recognize the importance of strong verbs in their writing.

TIP

Follow up by asking students to circle the verbs in a draft they're working on. Challenge them to replace vague or redundant verbs with more descriptive ones. Invite them to notice strong verbs in books they're reading.

SECOND Language LEARNERS

Play a lively game of Simon Says to help second-language learners develop vocabulary for verbs. Pair up students. Let them take turns giving each other Simon Says commands with one verb—for example, "Simon says, sit." Build up to two verb commands and then three. Performing the actions named by the verbs will help second-language learners remember their meaning. And everyone will enjoy the chance to move!

Action Name Tags

These name tags let students tell something about themselves as they learn more about verbs.

- Have each student choose a verb that starts with the same first letter as his or her name. (*Rob runs, Sara snowboards, Wendy whistles*) If students are new to learning verbs, you may want to post "verb banks" around your classroom that list a variety of verbs for students to choose from. An alternative is to have students each check their choice with you before proceeding, to make sure that they are making correct word choices.

- Give each student a sheet of sturdy paper. Have students fold their papers in half lengthwise to make name tags that will sit on their desks. Let them write their verbs and names on the paper and then illustrate themselves in action.

- When everyone's finished, let students take a walk around the room to appreciate the many action words that describe their classmates. Students will also enjoy using these name tags to point families in the right direction at open-school night.

Maryanne Frawley
Amery, Wisconsin

Fishing for Verbs

This pantomime activity begins with a fish bowl full of verbs.

Write verbs on slips of paper and place them in a fish bowl. Gather children in a circle to form a "pond," and pass the fish bowl to a volunteer. Have this student take a verb from the fish bowl, go to the center of the pond, and act out the word. Have the child who guesses the word take the next turn. Continue until everyone who wants a chance to act out a verb has had one.

For a variation on this activity, have students choose an adjective that begins with the first letter of their name and is also descriptive of themselves. Let children create name tags that combine the adjectives and their names.

When? Where? How?

"The southwest has never seen a snowstorm like this before ..." "The game-winning hit was over the fence..." "The governor made the announcement unexpectedly..." The newspaper is full of adverbs—words that tell when, where, or how something happened. Use newspapers to help children see how these describing words make writing stronger.

- Cut out newspaper stories and highlight adverbs that tell when, where, and how.

- Divide the class into small groups. Give each an article and ask students to read aloud the story. Then decide together what the highlighted words have in common.

- Bring students together to share their words and ideas. Create a three-column chart labeled "When," "Where," and "How." Ask students to record their words in the corresponding columns.

- Discuss how adverbs help make writing stronger. Then let children write a short news story about a school or family event. Encourage them to use adverbs to provide specific information that answers the questions when, where, or how.

TIP

Share students' news stories on the back of the weekly note home. You might be able to fit three or four on the back of each note. Over a period of a couple of months, each student will have a chance to share a story in this way.

The -*ly* Walk

Students will enjoy getting from one place to another in school with an activity that lets them act out adverbs.

Brainstorm words that end in -*ly* and tell how—for example, *happily, quickly, quietly, slowly, proudly,* and *casually.* Write these words on slips of paper and place them in a bag. Each day, when it's time to line up and go to lunch, recess, or a special, let a child choose a word and lead the class in moving down the hallway as described by the adverb. Add new words to the bag as students notice -*ly* adverbs in their reading.

Grammar-Gories

Students practice using parts of speech in this variation of a popular game.

🌀 Write the following categories on the chalkboard: Proper Noun, Common Noun, Past-Tense Verb, Future-Tense Verb, Adjective, Adverb.

🌀 Randomly choose a letter of the alphabet. (See Tip, left.) Demonstrate how to name a word for each category that starts with that letter. If the letter is *l*, you might use the word *London* for proper noun, *lake* for common noun, *licked* for past-tense verb, and so on.

🌀 Give each student a copy of page 45. Choose another random letter and have children record it on their paper in the appropriate space. Have children write down a word that starts with that letter for each category. The first person to fill in a word for each category calls out "Stop," at which point all students put down their pencils.

🌀 To award points, the student who finished first reads his or her word for proper noun. If no one else had that word, then the student who had a word for that category gets one point. If someone else had the same word, no points are awarded. The leader proceeds with words in each additional category and the scoring continues. At the end of the scoring, choose another letter and start a new round. For a cooperative scoring method, give everyone time to record a word for each category. Have students share their words, crossing off any that another student also has. How many different words did students come up with for each category?

Emily A. Olesch
Star of the Sea School
Virginia Beach, Virginia

TIP

Here's a fun way to randomly choose a letter of the alphabet: Have a student silently say the alphabet. After a moment, say "Stop." Use whatever letter of the alphabet the child was on as the target letter.

Flipping Over Parts of Speech

Children construct some amusing sentences with a flip book that targets parts of speech.

- Give each child multiple copies of page 46. Have children cut out the mini-book pages, stack them, and staple them at the top. Guide children in cutting the center dashed line of each page to make flaps.

- Brainstorm noun phrases with children and write them on the chalkboard—for example, "The ice cream," "Our teacher," "The hippopotamus," "The cat," "An alligator," "A boy," and "A girl." Do the same for verb phrases—for example, "won the race," "had the hiccups," "watched cartoons," "rode a roller coaster," "ate biscuits," "caught a mouse," and "suddenly screeched."

- Have students copy a noun phrase on the left flap of each page. Have them copy a verb phrase on the right flap of each page. Invite students to illustrate each flap.

- Show students how to flip the sections back and forth to build dozens of silly sentences—for example, with the phrases listed above, they can create these sentences and more: "An alligator ate biscuits." "The ice cream won the race." "The hippopotamus rode a roller coaster."

Karen K. Bjork
Portage Public Schools (retired)
Portage, Michigan

Cut-and-Paste Parts of Speech

Don't underestimate the power of a few art supplies, scissors, and a little glue! These simple materials bring life to this parts-of-speech lesson.

Invite students to search in magazines for nouns, verbs, adjectives, or other parts of speech you're studying. Have them cut out the words from headlines, advertisements, and other places where the type tends to be bigger. Let students use the words to form sentences, pasting them in place on construction paper, then adding illustrations. Students won't be able to make as many sentences as on a fill-in worksheet, but they will be much more likely to remember what they learn this way.

Maryanne Frawley
Amery, Wisconsin

Funny Fill-Ins

Mad Libs are a favorite with children. These fill-in-the-blank stories give students lots of practice with parts of speech, with very humorous results. Here's an activity that turns commercial worksheet pages into mini-Mad-Lib-like stories that are just as much fun.

Make a copy of several commercial grammar worksheets that ask children to complete sentences by filling in nouns, verbs, adjectives, adverbs, and so on. Use a correction pen to white out several additional words (nouns, verbs, adjectives, and adverbs) in each sentence—for example, an altered sentence might read _____ (noun that names a person) went to _____ (noun that names a place) to _____ (verb). Photocopy the revised worksheets and give one to each child. Pair up students, making sure each partner has a different sheet. Have students take turns asking their partners to supply the parts of speech called for in each sentence. (Partners should not be told the sentence before they supply the requested words.) Have students read completed sentences aloud for some silly results.

Janice Reutter
Boone, Iowa

Double-Agent Words

Students are often confused by words that have more than one usage—for example, words such as *can* that function both as a noun and a verb. Try this activity to familiarize students with such words and have some fun with wordplay.

◎ Write the following two sentences on the board: "Open the can of soup." "I can write my name." Ask students to identify the word that appears in both sentences. (*can*)

◎ Ask students to define the word *can* in each sentence. Guide students to notice that even though *can* looks, sounds, and is spelled the same in each sentence, it means different things. Ask students if *can* is a thing or an action in the first sentence. The second sentence?

◎ Share a couple of other examples of words that function as both nouns and verbs—for example, *present*, *saw*, and *heat*. Notice words that change pronunciation with use—for example: I got a *present* for my birthday. I will *present* my science project on Tuesday. You must *wind* this clock to make it work. The *wind* blew my hat off.

◎ Once students have the idea, let them team up to find their own double-agent words. Have students write sentences that use the word as a noun and a verb. Let students share their sentences, leaving blanks for the double-agent words. Can their classmates guess the word that fits in both sentences?

Janet Worthington-Samo
St. Clement School
Johnstown, Pennsylvania

I saw the saw on the workbench.

TIP

Make a game of using the dictionary to learn more about words with more than one usage. Challenge teams of students to find a word in the dictionary that has the most ways to use it. You might limit their search to words that start with, for example, the letter *a*. Being aware of multiple usage helps students with spelling, too.

Stand-Up Sentences

Students stand up and arrange themselves to make sentences. But they don't stay that way for long. Classmates can replace someone standing if they have the same part of speech!

Write a sentence on a sentence strip and cut it apart, word by word. Distribute the words to volunteers. Ask students to stand with their words and arrange themselves at the front of the room to make a sentence. From here, you can do a number of things. You can distribute other words and have students replace each other in the sentence. For example, ask, "Who could replace Sandy?" If Sandy has a noun, only those students also holding a noun could volunteer to replace her. Read the sentence aloud to see how it changes with the new student. You can also have students add adjectives and other parts of speech to the sentences.

Maryanne Frawley
Amery, Wisconsin

SECOND
Language
LEARNERS

In activities that ask students to build sentences with different parts of speech, try color-coding words to help second-language learners make choices. For example, write nouns in green, adjectives in purple, and verbs in red. Have students follow color patterns to put words together and build basic sentences—for example, sentences with a simple subject (*The dog*) and simple predicate (*barked*) would always be green and red.

Our Absolutely Awesome Alphabet

This collaborative bookmaking project has children playing with parts of speech from *A* to *Z*.

Share *The Absolutely Awful Alphabet*. (See below.) Then let each student choose a letter to create a class innovation on the book. (Leave the letter *Z* for the class to do together. If you have other letters left over, invite the principal, school nurse, and other members of the staff to contribute a page.) Before students begin writing, revisit various letters in the book and identify adjectives, nouns, verbs, and adverbs on each page. Have students meet with the classmate who has the next letter in the alphabet to create the transition from one letter to the next. Students can add illustrations to their pages, then put them together to make a book.

Literature LINK

The Absolutely Awful Alphabet

by Mordicai Gerstein (Harcourt Brace, 1999)

"A is an awfully arrogant Amphibian annoyed at…B who is a bashful, belching Bumpkin bullied by…" From *A* to *Z*, this book is full of adjectives, nouns, verbs, adverbs, and other "absolutely awful" parts of speech. Read it to see how choosing the right words can make for writing that paints unforgettable pictures.

Mustn't, Don't, Won't

Use poetry to help students learn more about using contractions in their writing.

Share Shel Silverstein's poem "Listen to the Mustn'ts," from *Where the Sidewalk Ends* (HarperCollins, 1974). Copy it on chart paper and let students highlight the contractions. Then set up a chart for recording the two words that make up the contractions, including *mustn't, don't, shouldn't,* and *won't.* Let students take turns recording contractions and the two words that make them.

Wendy Wise-Borg
Rider University
Lawrenceville, New Jersey

Animal Cracker Statements

Cooperative groups use animal crackers as springboards to construct declarative sentences.

⊙ Show children an animal cracker and ask them to identify what kind of animal it is. Write the animal's name on the board. (We'll say it's a lion for demonstration purposes.)

⊙ Ask children for information about the lion. ("The lion roars loudly.") Write this on the board. Then ask students to name more things that the lion does. ("The lion hunts. The lion sleeps. The lion eats.") Write these statements on the board, too.

⊙ Explain that a statement tells about something: It's more than one word; it is about one particular person or thing, in this case, a lion. But a statement also tells what that lion does. Invite children to point out the two parts of each sentence (subject and predicate).

⊙ Ask students how they can tell where one sentence ends and another begins. Let them see that statements always begin with a capital letter and end with a period. Now for the fun! Divide the class into groups and give each group a box of animal crackers. Have each group write statements about their animals and illustrate them. Display the sentences and illustrations, and invite students to find the subjects and predicates in each statement.

Janet Worthington-Samo
St. Clement School
Johnstown, Pennsylvania

Proofreading Like Pros

Proofreading is an obvious way for students to practice grammatical conventions, including punctuation, sentence structure, and word use. This activity challenges them to spot the errors even professional proofreaders missed!

- Explain to students that even though published material, such as a newspaper, gets proofread, mistakes still happen. Locate a newspaper article that contains a grammatical mistake, and place a transparency of it on the overhead. Challenge children to find the mistake.

- Ask children how many grammatical errors in published material they think they can find in one week. Provide the paper for review each day, and encourage children to look at home, too. You can also suggest other sources, such as kids' current events magazines and class or school newsletters.

- Have students highlight the mistakes, write the correction on an index card, and display both on a bulletin board. Take time to let students share their proofreading accomplishments, explaining the error and the correction. Encourage them to apply the same careful proofreading skills to their own work!

Beanillionaire Game

This game, piggybacked off the Millionaire game, means big beans for students who correctly answer grammar questions. Here's how it works.

Put together a set of grammar questions, each with four possible answers. (See sample, right.) Children might like to help come up with questions, too. Divide the class into groups. Explain that each team will be asked a series of questions about grammar and will be given four possible answers. Students on each team will take turns answering the questions. If children aren't sure of the answer, they may ask a buddy for help, ask to have two incorrect answers removed, or take an educated guess. If they answer correctly, they get 100 beans. Try to play the game more than once, having each team keep track of their beans from one round to the next. For more fun, let students use the beans to buy prizes (such as pencils and stickers) in an end-of-the-week auction.

Judy Wetzel
Bull Run Elementary
Centreville, Virginia

Sample Beanillionaire Question

What has the same meaning as *they're*?

a. there
b. their
c. they are
d. they there

If, And, But

This game challenges children to work together to form three-part sentences that use conjunctions.

I wanted to walk my dog | but | it was raining.

- On sentence strips, write sentences that use conjunctions. (Common conjunctions include *and, but, so, or,* and *because.*) Cut each sentence into three parts: the part before the conjunction, the conjunction, and the part after the conjunction. Make sure there is a sentence part for each child.

- Give each child part of a sentence. Explain that children need to search for two partners to complete their sentence. Because the goal is to have everyone be part of a sentence, children may need to rearrange themselves after forming their sentence in order to make other sentences work.

- Once everyone has found partners, let children read aloud the sentences. Ask students to tell how each conjunction connects the other two parts.

Connect Two

Children pair up to write sentences on a selected topic, then see how fast they can connect them using conjunctions.

Brainstorm topics that can generate lots of discussion—for example, favorite after-school activities, bedtime, cafeteria food, or homework. Write the topics on slips of paper, then let a volunteer randomly choose one. Ask each child to write a sentence on that topic. When everyone has a sentence, have children pair up and try to join their sentences with a conjunction. (You can write common conjunctions on the chalkboard for reference.) To make the activity more challenging, children might like to set a timer. Can they combine their sentences in under ten seconds? Let children read aloud their combined sentences and tell why they chose the particular conjunction.

Punctuation Bounce

A ball gives students a hands-on lesson in using end punctuation and capital letters.

Gather students in a group and pull out a basketball. Begin bouncing it around the group, and ask children what the ball is doing. (Bounce it hard so it rebounds, at least as high as your head.) When they reply "The ball bounces up high," ask what punctuation mark the ball reminds them of. Establish that "When you put a period (the basketball) at the end of a sentence, it will bounce up high indicating the need for a capital letter to begin the next word." Silly, but it helps students remember this new skill!

Charlotte Sassman
Alice Carlson Applied Learning Center
Fort Worth, Texas

Literature LINK

Bing Bang Boing

by Douglas Florian (Harcourt Brace, 1994)

This delightful collection of poems includes the eight-line "Commas" (see page 47), which gives children a great visual for remembering what this punctuation mark looks like—it's the one with claws! For a related activity, see page 32.

TIP

Tests that include sections on conventions of language often include a passage with punctuation and/or spelling mistakes for children to edit. Children might be asked to highlight errors, then write the appropriate punctuation above them. To help students organize their approach to such a task, teach them the "Beginning and Ending" strategy: Check the beginning of sentences for capitals, then check the end of sentences for ending punctuation.

Commas With Claws

After sharing the poem "Commas" with students
(see Literature Link, page 31), let them bring their own
commas to life.

- Share "Commas," by Douglas Florian, along with the illustrations that accompany the poem. (See page 47.) Ask students why they think the poet likens commas to claws.

- With this visual in mind, let students create commas that are as alive as those in the poem. They might turn them into catlike creatures, even dress them up in the "comma pajamas" mentioned in the poem.

- Let students find commas in books they're reading. Invite them to share ideas about how commas can help make sentences easier to read and understand. For example, writers use commas to separate ideas and items in a series, to separate cities from states and months from dates, and to set apart speakers from quotations.

- Have students find an example of a comma used in one of these ways and write the sentence next to their creative comma picture. Create a display that students can easily refer to when they're wondering about using commas in their own writing.

Quiet Quotations

This quiet activity is surprisingly fun—it teaches the use of quotation marks without anyone speaking at all!

Pair up students after teaching a lesson on using quotations. Have students write back and forth to each other four or five times (for about 10–15 minutes), using questions and answers with quotations and dialogue tags. What makes the activity really fun is requiring that no one speak aloud at all. Students must write everything! (Keep the focus on using quotation marks, and off spelling and other skills for now.)

Charlotte Sassman
Alice Carlson Applied Learning Center
Fort Worth, Texas

Comic Captions

Funny photos bring out the comedians in children while teaching about quotation marks.

Look for funny photos in newspapers and magazines. Invite students to find them, too. Cut out the photos and display them a few at a time on a bulletin board. Provide copies of the word bubbles on page 48. Let children use the word bubbles (with quotation marks) to tell what the person in the photo is saying. Have children display their word bubbles next to the corresponding photos for an amusing classroom display.

Macaroni Marks

Elbow macaroni becomes a memorable manipulative in a literature-based activity that teaches the use of quotation marks.

Copy a familiar text (a selection from the Frog and Toad series, by Arnold Lobel, works well) on chart paper. Leave out the punctuation marks. Lead a discussion about where the periods should go. After letting children take turns filling them in, talk about what Frog and Toad are saying. Guide children to notice that it's difficult to follow who is saying what without proper punctuation. Demonstrate the use of quotation marks by gluing two pieces of elbow macaroni at the beginning of the first conversation. Ask children to tell where the end of that thought is. Place two more pieces of macaroni there. Continue, asking children where pieces of the dialogue begin and end and gluing macaroni in place accordingly. Children will remember that "quotation marks are like macaroni" as they continue to place macaroni where each quotation mark would go.

Charlotte Sassman
Alice Carlson Applied Learning Center
Fort Worth, Texas

For dozens of displays that build grammar skills and more, see *Interactive Bulletin Boards: Language Arts*, by Judy Meagher and Joan Novelli (Scholastic, 1998).

Name _____   Date _____

Rhyming People, Places, Things

Read the nouns. Fill in the blank with a rhyming
noun or noun phrase. The first one shows you how!

1. A can, a pan, and a ___man named Dan_____ .

2. A stack, a track, and a _____ .

3. A bank, a prank, and a _____ .

4. A jet, a net, and a pet named _____ .

5. A mop, a drop, and a sign that says _____ .

6. A string, a ring, and a king who can _____ .

7. A sock, a rock, and a clock that goes tick _____ .

8. Our town, a crown, and a clown in a _____ .

TRY THIS!

Create your own rhyming noun set. Write it here. Leave a blank so a
classmate can fill in a noun.

Name _____   Date _____

Noun-a-Morphs

Dear Family,
We're studying parts of speech in class—including nouns and proper nouns. Try this activity with your child to teach about nouns that need capital letters. To complete the activity, your child needs to "morph" each noun to make it a proper noun, then highlight each capital letter.

Noun		Proper Noun
author		Dr. Seuss
boy		
girl		
street		
day		
month		
book		
city		
state		
country		

Name _____ Date _____

Alphabet Countdown

A	N
B	O
C	P
D	Q
E	R
F	S
G	T
H	U
I	V
J	W
K	X
L	Y
M	Z

Best-Ever Activities for Grades 2–3: Grammar Scholastic Professional Books

Name _____ Date _____

Pronoun Bingo

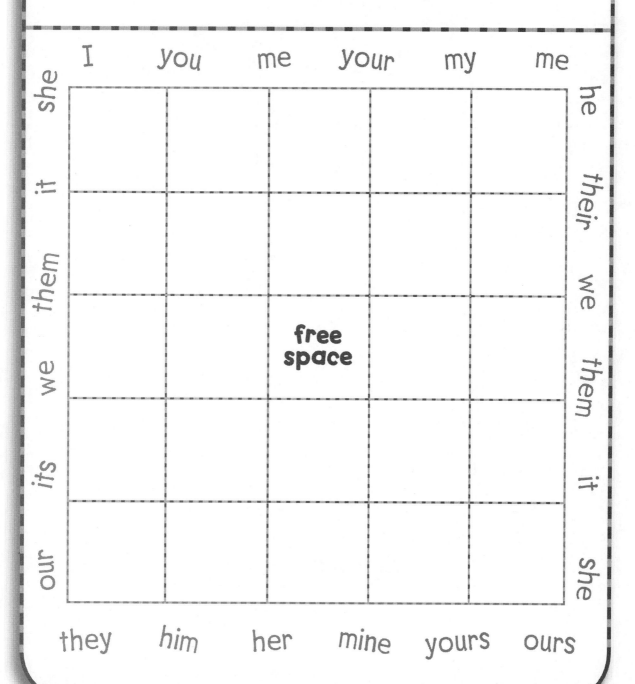

	I	you	me	your	my	me	
she							he
it							their
them			free space				we
we							them
its							it
our							she
	they	him	her	mine	yours	ours	

Name _____ Date _____

Adjective Detectives

What's in my sock?
Read the clues and
then guess!

Clue 1 _____

Clue 2 _____

Clue 3 _____

Lift the flap to
check your answer.

Tape flap here.

Best-Ever Activities for Grades 2–3: Grammar   Scholastic Professional Books

Name _____   Date _____

Adjective Olympics
1st Place in

_____

Awarded to

_____

on

_____

Name _____ Date _____

Adjective

_____

Synonyms

_____

_____

_____

4

I'm in a thesaurus,
Look and see!
Here are some adjectives
That tell about me!

by _____

1

3

2

_____

_____

_____

Synonyms

Adjective

_____

_____

_____

Synonyms

Adjective

Name _____ Date _____

Colorful Caterpillars Grow Long

Name _____   Date _____

Adjectives About Me

I am a [ ] boy.   [ ] girl.

My eyes are _____ .

My hair is _____ .

I am _____ than a _____ .

I am _____ than a _____ .

I am more _____ than a _____ .

I am good at _____ .

I am better at _____ .

I am best at _____ .

Tape flap here.

Who am I? [   ]

Name _____ Date _____

Dunk, Dive, Slide!

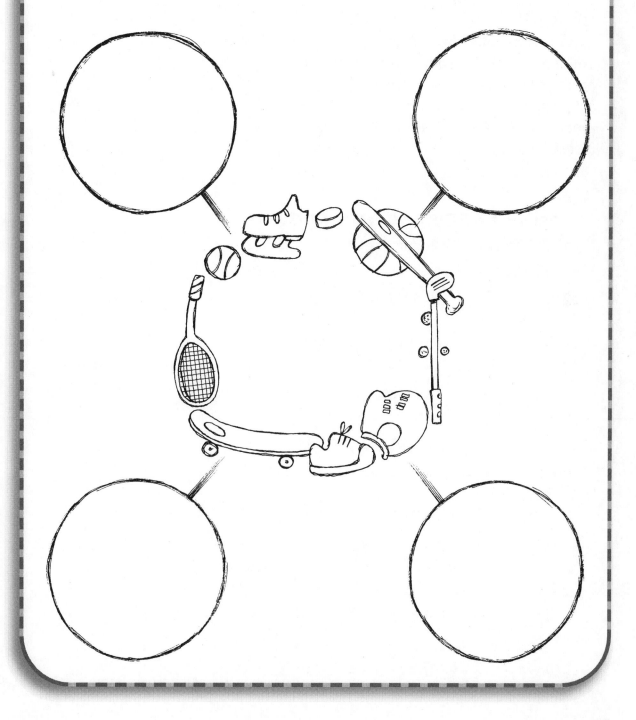

Name _____ Date _____

Clap, Wiggle, Stomp

Dear Families,

Music is a natural with children, and integrating it with skills and concepts in other parts of the curriculum can help reinforce learning in memorable ways. Here's an action-packed song you can sing with your child to practice verbs. Repeat the song to try the new actions (listed below).

If You're Happy and You Know It

If you're happy and you know it, clap your hands,

If you're happy and you know it, clap your hands,

If you're happy and you know it,
and you really want to show it,

If you're happy and you know it, clap your hands.

Actions for Our New Verses

_____

_____

_____

_____

TRY THIS!

Can your family think of a new action for the song? Write it here. Sing it together!

Best-Ever Activities for Grades 2–3: Grammar Scholastic Professional Books

Name _____

Date _____

Grammar-Gories

Proper Noun	Common Noun	Past-Tense Verb	Future-Tense Verb	Adjective	Adverb	Letter

Best-Ever Activities for Grades 2–3: Listening & Speaking   Scholastic Professional Books

ACTIVITY PAGE

Name _____ Date _____

Flipping Over
Parts of Speech

Staple

Staple

Best-Ever Activities for Grades 2–3: Grammar   Scholastic Professional Books

Name _____   Date _____

Commas

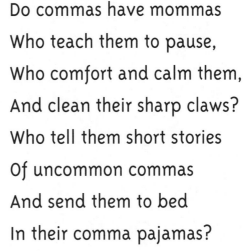

Do commas have mommas
Who teach them to pause,
Who comfort and calm them,
And clean their sharp claws?
Who tell them short stories
Of uncommon commas
And send them to bed
In their comma pajamas?

—Douglas Florian

Best-Ever Activities for Grades 2–3: Grammar Scholastic Professional Books

Name _____ Date _____

Comic Captions